THE PROOF
OF GOD

BY DOUGLAS SUMMERS

DORRANCE
PUBLISHING CO
EST. 1920
PITTSBURGH, PENNSYLVANIA 15238

Dorrance Publishing Co
585 Alpha Drive
Suite 103
Pittsburgh, PA 15238
Visit our website at *www.dorrancebookstore.com*

ISBN: 979-8-89211-950-4
eISBN: 979-8-89211-699-2

THE PROOF
OF GOD

CONTENTS

CHAPTER ONE
WHAT HAS HAPPENED TO CHRISTIANITY IN AMERICA?

The answer is, our political system. Our founding fathers, George Washington and Benjamin Franklin, along with others, belonged to an organization called the Masonic order. They were concerned about the power of the Catholic Church. Why were they nervous or afraid of the Catholic Church? Some historians thought that the organization called the Masonic order came about because in the year 1000 the Catholic

Church decided, for some reason, to require a vow of celibacy (which is abstaining from sex) for the Catholic priests. So married priests were expelled out of the priesthood. This obviously angered them. It was thought by some historians that this caused the start of the organization called the Masonic order.

To show you how powerful this organization is in America, since I was born, in 1938, there have been eight different presidents or more that belonged to this organization. Not only that, but of the thirteen colonies of the original United States, three of them had governors also belonging to the Masonic order. Also, up until recently, 25 percent or more of both the Congress and the Senate were members of this organization. So in order to protect <u>themselves</u> from the power of the Catholic Church, possessed in Europe, our founding fathers created a Constitution and a Bill of Rights to protect <u>themselves</u> from the power of that organization. Unfortunately, it also gave the American people the freedom of religion and the right to believe in anything they wished religiously. The Constitution and the Bill of Rights did protect our founding fathers from the power of the Catholic Church, but they also gave the American public the freedom to choose <u>or create</u> any religion they wished. With this freedom of religion, they could not only be a Hindu, a Muslim, a Buddhist or any other existing religion that they wished; they also could <u>create their own religion</u>, and within a few decades of becoming a country many people started to create different religions that never existed before. So the Constitution and the Bill of Rights did protect our founding fathers from the power of the Catholic Church that they had in Europe; it also gave the American people the right and the freedom to create any religion they wished.

This began what American historians refer to as <u>the great evangelistic period</u> in America. Up to this point in time, the Catholic Church was basically the only church available for Christians. However, because of the Bill of Rights and our Constitution, from the early 1800s new and many unknown religions that had never existed before began to emerge and all of them claiming to be Christian. By using our freedom of religion and the book called <u>the Holy Bible</u>, which was created by the Catholic Church in the 1500s, you could make or create any religion that you wished. In 1836 a man named Joseph Smith started the Mormon religion and introduced, secretly, behind closed doors, <u>polygamy</u> (a man having more than one wife). Why? Because polygamy was in the book called the Holy Bible, <u>in the Old Testament</u>. Other organizations followed. In 1844 the Jehovah's Witnesses Church began as well, and this has continued until today. Because of our right of freedom of religion, we can create any new religion. Even churches that talk in unknown languages, which is also in the Bible, and others handling poisonous snakes, which is also in that book as well, were created. Because all of these ideas came from that one book and they all claimed to be Christian. By Americans using that book called the Holy Bible and our freedom of religion, Christianity became overwhelmingly diversified in America.

Every group of American citizens had the right to create any church they wished. How could this have happened? The answer is when you study other religions around the world, it becomes obvious that there is consistency in their places of worship because there is only one authority for each religion. Moses speaks and teaches Judaism, and when you go from one synagogue to another their religious teachings are consistent and the same. This also applies to Mohammed; he is the authority for Muslims, and the same is true when you go from one mosque to another. This is also true for Buddhists. Buddha is the absolute authority for Buddhists, and like the other religious organizations Buddhist temples are consistent and the same. However, there does not seem to be an absolute authority for Christianity. Christians don't seem to have just one leader. By using this entire book called the Holy Bible, which was created five hundred years ago and has many different writers in it and two separate religions in it, many <u>pseudo-Christian churches</u> were created. American churches have many different leaders, from Moses, who started the Jewish religion four thousand years ago, to Paul and beyond, and this has led to all of these so-called Christian churches that exist today in America. You can be a Catholic, a Mormon, a Jehovah's Witness, a Baptist, or any hundreds of other so-called Christian churches. As different as they all are from each other, they can all justify their false religious beliefs by using the same source, this book called the Holy Bible.

CHAPTER TWO
IS THE BIBLE THE WORD OF GOD ACCORDING TO JESUS?

At this point I would like to bring to your attention two definitions. First, the definition of a <u>Biblicist</u>. This is an expert on the Holy Bible <u>or a person who interprets the Holy Bible literally.</u> <u>These are the people who believe that the entire Bible is the Word of God. These are those people who declare that the Bible is the Word of God,</u> which Jesus will, and has, <u>flatly denied</u>. Second, a <u>Christian</u> is a person who believes that

Jesus Christ was the promised Messiah of the old Jewish Law, and here is the important part of that definition: <u>They base their religious beliefs upon the teachings of Jesus Christ.</u> Not the teachings of Moses or Paul or any other person in the Bible. The Gospels are the only place in the entire Bible that Jesus speaks or teaches his doctrine. The Catholic Bible is literally over 90-percent <u>non-Christian</u> and the King James Version of the Bible is not much better. How could the Christian community come up with this cliché, that the Holy Bible is the Word of God, since there are <u>two separate religions in this book that do not agree with each other?</u>

Most Christians base their religious beliefs on that entire Bible, but unfortunately the Bible is only 10-percent Christian. This allows every church to be different and unique. They are able to take from those two religions that are in the Bible anything they wish, from a little Christianity when it is convenient to as much Judaism as they like. This is how Joseph Smith and the Mormon founding fathers justified the practice of polygamy (a man having more than one wife); after all, polygamy was in the Old Testament of the Bible. Jim Jones was also having sex with men and children because that's also in the Old Testament of the Bible. However, a Christian should base their religious beliefs upon the teachings of Jesus, recorded in the Gospels of the <u>New Testament</u> only. Christ alone and his teachings are recorded in four books of that Holy Bible: Matthew, Mark, Luke and John. By using these four books only, all of these churches or religions created in America could not exist. Jesus does speak in the book of Revelation; however, it is his ideas or his thoughts, and he will admit in the Gospels that nobody knows when the end of the world is going to happen, except for his Father only. If you read from the entire Bible, it will mislead you from the teachings of Jesus, and he preaches this throughout the Gospels.

First, let's examine the Jewish theologian's point of view regarding the Old Testament being the Word of God. These people are the absolute authority for the Jewish religion.

They not only know the Jewish religion, but they also know the history of the Jewish people. Those theologians are quick to point out that their Bible, or the Old Testament, is not the Word of God. The first five books of the Old Testament are Moses-inspired writings. This is the Torah and the only part that Jews consider as inspired writings. The rest of their Bible is broken down into three different sections, or subjects, which are the history of the Jewish people, having nothing to do with any doctrine of the Jewish law and being nothing more than a historical record of the Jewish people. The other two parts of their Bible are Psalms and Proverbs, which are poetry and correctness, again having nothing to do with the Jewish religion. In order to understand how and why the Christian Bible came into existence, you must know a little history.

When Jesus was born, the Jews had already finished their Bible, or the Old Testament, which took them five hundred years to put together. In the New Testament, it is recorded that Jesus understood the Jewish Bible or the Old Testament very well, because he was a Jew himself. Now it was the Christian's turn to create their Bible. The year was approximately 325 A.D. By this time, the center of the Christian church had moved from Jerusalem or the Jewish community to Rome and is known today as the Vatican. A group of Catholic officials near Africa called the Council of Hippo submitted a large amount of books or writings that they thought pertained to the story of Jesus. Starting with Moses and many other writers and ending with the book of Revelation, the Vatican began to consider which of these books or writings to accept for their Christian Bible. There was a Catholic priest named <u>Father Conti</u> and when he saw this gigantic stack of material, he stated that all of this material was not necessary. He declared that the only part of that material <u>Christians required</u> for their spiritual guidance were <u>the four books of the Gospels,</u> which were the books of Matthew, Mark, Luke and John, <u>and he was right</u>. However, his suggestion was ignored and the Vatican began to select what they thought were the important parts of that gigantic stack of literature. This started a process of voting by individual levels of the Catholic Church. They would read, discuss, debate and <u>vote</u> on these books, and this process went on for no less than 1200 years.

An interesting note: The Anti-Christ was once described this way. The Anti-Christ will be born of politics, and that's exactly how the Holy Bible was created. That Bible, along with Americans' right of freedom of religion, created all of these so-called Christian churches in America today that are as different as Catholics are from snake handlers and Mormons are from Baptists. This is why Christians should only use the Gospels for their religious guidance. The Bible was finally finished and published in the 1500s and was immediately criticized by many scholars that studied these books or writings and disagreed with the Vatican's selections of the books they chose.

When this book finally got published in the 1500s, a Catholic priest named Martin Luther (not to be confused with Martin Luther King) broke away from the Vatican and started the Lutheran church. I believe that this was the first organization that deviated from the Catholic Church. So this book, called the Holy Bible, did not bring about unity; it brought about division in the Christian community. However, these two organizations are very similar and almost identical. <u>Father Conti was correct;</u>

Christians only need the Gospels for their religious guidance. After all, the Gospels are the only place in the entire Bible that Jesus speaks his doctrine. Jesus does comment on the book of Revelation, which is a story about the end of the world; however, Jesus Christ admitted in the book of Matthew, chapter 24, verse 36, he says of <u>that day and hour</u> knoweth no man, no not the angels in heaven, but my Father only. Jesus also warns his own followers not to seek a sign, and that's what the book of Revelation is. Jesus doesn't want people to ponder the end of the world. What a morbid thought it is, to ponder the end of the world.

In the book of Matthew, chapter 12, verse 30, it says: "But he (Jesus) answered and said unto them an evil and adulterous generation seek after a sign, and there shall no sign be given to it." What a waste of time for some Christians to literally study this. Nobody knows when the end of the world will come, and all the book of Revelation is, <u>is a sign</u> and it should be ignored. Now this brings us to a question, is the Holy Bible the Word of God, according to our Lord and Savior Jesus Christ? The answer is it can't be, because the Holy Bible has two different religions in it that disagree with each other. There is the Old Testament, which is the Jewish religion, and it is followed by the New Testament, which is the Christian religion. These two religions have very little in common. If you are a Jew and believe in Judaism, you go to a synagogue, and if you are a Christian, you go to what you think is one of the Christian organizations. Simply put, Jews go to their synagogues and Christians don't; they go to what they think a Christian church is. This alone should completely discredit the cliché that <u>the Bible is the Word of God.</u> Does God respect Judaism or does God respect his son's religion, called Christianity? What do you think? These two religions do not agree with each other. The experts of both the Jewish religion and the Christian religion agree that the Holy Bible cannot be the Word of God because these two religions are incompatible with each other.

The Apostle John wrote in chapter 1, verse 17: "For the law was given by

Moses but <u>grace and truth</u> came by Jesus Christ." So according to John the apostle, Moses gave the law of Judaism, but the <u>truth and grace of Christianity came by Jesus Christ. John also wrote that Jesus said in chapter 14, verse 6: "I am the way (and that way is his doctrine that can guide us to heaven), the truth (that was not given by Moses or Paul or anyone else),</u> and the life (and this is life eternal)." Then Jesus goes on to say something all Christians should listen to: "<u>No man cometh unto the father, but by me.</u>" So much for Moses. Jesus knew that his doctrine would lead us to heaven, Moses' doctrine won't. He wasn't talking about believing in him as the Christ, but believing in his doctrine. Why? In the book of Matthew, chapter 11, verse 27, Jesus says: "All things are delivered unto me of my father." Can Moses or Paul or anyone else in the Bible say that? Jesus was talking about his doctrine that he got from his Father in heaven. He goes on to explain why you should only listen to him: "No man knoweth the son but the father (and here's the important part of that Scripture), neither knoweth any man the father, save the son, and he to whom soever the son reveal him." Only Jesus knew God. That statement included everybody from Moses to Paul and beyond. Nobody knew God like Jesus did. Neither Moses nor anyone else in the Bible was talking for God; they were only giving their own opinion. Remember the word "Gospel"? According to the dictionary, it means "<u>the truth</u>." Jesus criticized much of what is in the Old Testament many times. He wasn't criticizing the Word of God, but was criticizing what was in the Old Testament. This is the Jewish Bible or the Jewish religion. He warned his followers not to combine these two religions.

First, in the book of Matthew, chapter 9, verse 16, Jesus says: "No man putteth a piece of new cloth (which is Christianity or the New Testament) onto an old garment (which is the Old Testament or the Jewish religion)." This Scripture is repeated in the book of Mark, chapter 2, verse 21; however, in the book of Luke, chapter 5, verse 36, Luke explains <u>why</u> you shouldn't combine these two religions. Luke writes that Jesus spoke a parable unto them: "<u>No man putteth a piece of new cloth</u> (the New Testament) upon an old garment (the Old Testament); if otherwise then both the new maketh a rent (which means to rip apart)," and the piece that was taken out of the new (which is the New Testament) <u>agreed not with the old</u> (which is the Old Testament or the Jewish religion). They are two different religions and they should not be combined, and that's exactly what the Holy Bible did. So the cliché that states that the Bible is the Word of God is wrong, according to Jesus Christ. There are major differences in these two religions. How clearly can Jesus explain this to us? The two religions are incompatible with each other in many ways.

Let's examine a few examples of the differences between these two religions. In the book of John, chapter 8, verse 3, it is recorded that scribes and Pharisees brought unto Jesus a woman taken in adultery and when they had set her in the midst, John says in verse 4: "They (the Jews that brought Mary Magdalena to Jesus) said unto him, 'Master, this woman was taken in adultery in the very act.'" Verse 5: Now Moses <u>in the law</u> commanded us that such should be stoned (murdered) but what saith thou. This is a place in the Gospels where Jesus had to put his foot down and make a stand against Moses' opinion and the Jewish religion. The Jewish leaders that brought Mary to Jesus were hoping that Jesus would criticize Moses openly, in order to get him in trouble with other Jewish leaders. What did Jesus have to say about Moses commanding that a woman who commits adultery should be killed? Verse 7: "So when they continued asking him, he lifted up himself and said unto them, 'He that is without sin among you, let him first cast a stone at her,'" disagreeing with Moses and the Old Testament. With scriptures like this, how could the Bible be the Word of God? And why was this punishment only given to a woman? So either Moses was wrong or Jesus was wrong. Jesus knew all people are sinners and worthy of forgiveness. Thank God the Jews that brought Mary to Jesus were decent men that knew that this rule of Moses was wrong as well. Today these churchgoers should remember that as well. Christians should stop looking at sins in others, and should look for sins within themselves.

Moses said that she should be killed, which is strange because when God supposedly gave Moses the 10 Commandments, one of those commandments was "<u>Thou shalt not kill</u>." However, Jesus forgave her. How many women were put to death because of Moses and his religion? I am not antisemitic, but I am very much anti-killing women, especially for something a man does also. Thank God he sent his son to us to denounce this Jewish rule. How can someone believe the Bible is the Word of God, with contradictions like this that are in the same book? How could the entire Bible be the Word of God? What did Jesus say regarding who you should listen to or believe in? The answer is literally scattered throughout the Gospels many times and in many ways. In the book of John, chapter 6, verse 31, the Jews were challenging Jesus with "Our Father did eat manna (which is bread) in the desert, as it is written, God gave them bread from heaven to eat." This demonstrates what Jesus thought regarding Moses and his religion. Because God provided them with edible bread in the desert, they thought that somehow God favored Moses in some way, and they were right, but Jesus corrected them with this. Verse 32: "Then Jesus said unto them, 'Verily, verily, I say unto you, <u>Moses gave you not that bread from heaven,</u> but my father gives you <u>the true bread</u> (which is Jesus' doctrine).'" Verse 51: Jesus goes on to say: <u>"I am that living bread which came down from heaven."</u> Is that clear enough?

Then Jesus says: "If any man <u>eat of this bread</u> (his doctrine, and we should all eat that bread), <u>he shall live forever."</u> He put it another way in the same book of John, chapter 10, verse 8: <u>"All that ever came before me are thieves and robbers."</u> He's talking about the Old Testament and Moses. How clear can Jesus be? Jesus goes on to say: "But the sheep did not hear them" (thousands of Jews believed in Jesus and his doctrine). Christians and many Jews are the sheep, and we should not hear the voice of Moses or the Old Testament. Jesus' doctrine can lead us to heaven, Moses' doctrine can lead us to hell. Then Jesus goes on to say something all Christians should listen to: "<u>No man cometh unto the father but by me.</u>" That is not necessarily believing in Jesus as the Messiah or the Christ, <u>but you must live his doctrine.</u> In the book of Matthew, chapter 11, verse 27, Jesus explains why you should only listen to him and no one else. Jesus says: "<u>All things are delivered unto me of my father.</u>" Then he says: "No man knows the father but the son and to whomsoever the son will reveal him." Moses didn't know God as Jesus knew him nor did he claim to. Jesus and his doctrine are the truth and the pathway to heaven, not the entire Bible. Indeed, the Bible will mislead you from things that Jesus taught. In the book of John, chapter 6, verse 29, the Jews asked Jesus to give them a sign. Jesus answered and said: "Unto them, this is the work of God that ye may believe on him <u>whom he has sent</u>" (he was referring to himself). People who believe in the entire Bible as the Word of God have never studied this book. Jesus never shared his position with anyone. Did Moses have a close relationship with God as Jesus did?

In the book of Deuteronomy, Moses writes in chapter 24, verse 1: "When a man hath taken a wife, and married her, and it come to pass that she finds <u>no favor in his eyes</u> because he has found some uncleanliness in her, let him write her a bill of divorcement, and give it in her hands and send her out of his house." This demonstrates the disrespect that Moses and the male Jews had for women back in those days. I'd like to believe that the Jewish men have outgrown that particular rule of Moses. Men do not have the right to divorce a woman for any reason, according to Jesus, except if she doesn't stop having sex with other men. Men who believe in that rule of Moses today we refer to as chauvinistic. Verse 2 says: "And when she is departed out of his house she may go and be another man's wife." How generous of a man. Jesus will explain how ridiculous this rule is. Is this true? Was Moses right? Was this what

God wanted? The Jews approached Jesus with this very question in the book of Matthew, chapter 5, verse 31. Jesus said: "It hath been said, 'Whosoever shall put away his wife let him give her a writing of divorcement.'" This was what Moses thought, did Jesus share that same opinion? He said in verse 32: "But I say unto you, that whosoever shall put away his wife saving for the cause of <u>fornication</u> (meaning if she can't stop having sex with other men) causes her to commit adultery." Do you understand? If a man divorces a woman for any reason, even though he gives her the right to become someone else's wife, she will be committing adultery, according to the law of Moses. Jesus goes on to say: "And whosoever shall marry her that is divorced (like the creep that divorced her and threw her out of his house) commits adultery." What he was explaining to them is marriage is a lot more complicated and involved than Moses thought. He goes on to say: "and the man who divorces her marries another woman, he's also committing adultery, <u>according to the law of Moses</u>." God believes in the sanctity of marriage. Jesus completely disagreed with Moses. I wonder what a Biblicist (a person who believes in the entire Bible <u>as the Word of God</u>) would say to that? Why people dogmatically continue to say that the Bible is the Word of God, when according to Jesus it is clearly not, is beyond me.

Jesus explains how Moses went

wrong in the book of Matthew, chapter 19, verse 7: "They (the Jews) say unto him, 'Why did Moses then command to give a writing of divorcement, and to put her away?'" Verse 8: "He (Jesus) saith unto them, 'Moses <u>because of the hardness of your hearts</u> suffered you to put away your wives.'" This shows that Moses was giving his own opinion, not getting directions from God, according to Jesus. And this is the important part. Jesus says: "<u>But from the beginning it was not so</u>." So much for the Bible being the Word of God according to Jesus. The only way that the Bible could possibly be the Word of God is that Jesus must be lying. This is not an isolated case where Jesus disagrees with Moses. In the book of Exodus, Moses writes in chapter 21, verse 23: "If any <u>mischief</u> (when one person harms another) follows, then thou shalt give" verse 24: "<u>eye for eye, tooth for tooth, foot for foot, and life for life.</u>" In simple terms, whatever someone does to you, do it back to them. This is Moses and Judaism, is it Christian? Jesus responded in the book of Matthew, chapter 5, verse 38: "He (Jesus) said, 'Ye have heard that it has been said an eye for an eye and a tooth for tooth <u>but I say unto you that ye resist not evil but whosoever shall smite thee on the right cheek turned to him the other also.</u>'" <u>Jesus was a pacifist. This is a hard rule that must be followed if you're a Christian.</u> This is the reason that as a Christian you must ignore the teachings of Moses and the Jewish religion. Jesus disagrees with Moses and the Jewish religion many times. These two religions should have never been combined with each other, but the Catholic Church did when they create that book called <u>the Holy Bible</u>. Between that book and the American rights to create their own religion, it has destroyed Christianity. Christians are not the enemies of the Jews, they are our brothers, as much as all people are; however, we are just different. Each religion follows a leader; we just follow our leader, Jesus Christ, <u>and his doctrine</u>. A Christian cannot believe in Christianity and also believe in Judaism. They are two different religions and they should have never been combined together. This is why Christians don't go to synagogues and

Jews do not attend what is considered a Christian church.

There are many examples in the Gospels where Jesus disagrees with the Old Testament. How does a Biblicist live with the contradictions that are in the Bible? They just dogmatically repeat that false cliché that the Bible is the Word of God and Jesus said over and over that his disciples or followers should only listen to him and his doctrine. The Catholic Church has committed many atrocities that are well documented throughout history. The Crusades, the Inquisitions and much, much more, but when they created the book called <u>the Holy Bible</u>, this was the greatest atrocity or blasphemy that the Catholic Church has ever committed, <u>in my opinion</u>. Just consider the amount of damage that was caused when the Catholic Church created <u>the Holy Bible</u> and the American Government gave us the right of freedom of religion and what this has done to Christianity in America. Before America was created, there was only one church, the Catholic Church. Wow! Have things changed. The Holy Bible places the teachings of Jesus in the Gospels with so much other literature that is not Christian that Jesus and his doctrine get ignored. I have no idea when or where the cliché of <u>the Bible is the Word of God</u> came from, but it certainly didn't come from Jesus. So why do some Christians believe in the entire Bible as the Word of God? Ignorance.

Jesus says in his doctrine repeatedly, many times in the Gospels, that you should only believe in him and his teachings. In the book of John, chapter 10, verse 27, Jesus says: "My sheep <u>hear my voice and I know them and they follow me</u>." Not other men. Do you follow Jesus or do you follow the Bible? A Christian doesn't follow Moses or Paul or anyone else in the Bible; they only hear the voice of Jesus. For Christians, this is the only path to haven. A Biblicist follows whoever they want in that book called the Holy Bible. This book has caused a lot of damage to Christianity. <u>Father Conti was correct</u> six hundred years ago when he said, "<u>We only need the Gospels for guidance.</u>" In the book of John, chapter 18, verse 37, Jesus talked to Pontius Pilate (the judge at Jesus' trial) and the conversation went like this: "'Therefore,' said Pontius Pilate unto him, 'art thou a king?' Jesus answered, 'Thou saith that I am a king. <u>To this end was I born</u> and for this cause, came I unto the world, that I should bear witness unto <u>the truth</u>.'" Jesus was the king of the Jews and the truth was only taught by him. He goes on to say: "<u>Everyone that is of the truth heareth my voice</u>" (they don't hear the voice of Moses or anyone else in the Bible). Christians only hear God's guidance when they listen to Jesus and his doctrine.

In the book of John, chapter 8, verse 31, then said Jesus to those Jews who believed in him: "If ye continue <u>in my word</u> (not the word of Moses or

Paul or any other voice in the Holy Bible), <u>then are ye my disciples indeed."</u> That was the requirement for a Jew or anybody that wanted to become a Christian. To continue in <u>his word</u>. They had to accept the doctrine of Christianity and reject what Moses thought or anybody else in the Bible. According to Jesus, to be his follower you should only listen to what he says. When you begin to listen to all the others in the Bible besides Jesus, you will be led astray. All other men give their opinions and they don't speak for God. In the book of John, chapter 10, verse 16, Jesus says: "And other sheep I have, which are not of this fold (that's us) them also I must bring and <u>they shall hear my voice</u>." How many times does Jesus have to say "<u>only</u>

listen to me"? They won't hear the voice of Moses or anyone else in the Bible; they will only hear the voice and the teachings of Jesus Christ. Then he goes on to say "and there shall be one fold and one shepherd." Do you consider all of these churches in America as one fold? Or do you consider the voice of the Pope, Jimmy Swaggart, Robert Schuller, Jerry Falwell, David Karesh and Jim Jones as one shepherd? Do you consider all of these churches in America one fold? Consider all of the so-called Christian churches that exist today in America: Catholics, Mormons, Jehovah's Witnesses, Baptists, churches that talk in tongues, and churches that handle poisonous snakes one fold. If all churches only listened to Jesus, there would not be all of these pseudo-Christian religions that exist today in America, and they are spreading their false doctrine that they get from the Bible or even other literature, like the Book of Mormon, all over the world. That Bible has created thousands of religions that declare that the Bible is the Word of God (which it clearly is not, according to Jesus).

In the book of John, chapter 14, verse 15, Jesus says: "If ye love me keep my commandments." Listening to Jesus and his teachings is the only path to salvation, according to Jesus himself. There is so much literature of other men in that book called the Holy Bible that you can make any church you want out of it, and it can be as different as the Catholics are from the Mormons or people who handle snakes are from Jehovah's Witnesses or people who talk in tongues are as different as the Baptists. After all, these things are all in that book called the Holy Bible. Nowhere in the Bible does Jesus ever say to his followers that they should listen to anyone else besides him. It's only through his teachings that the truth of Christianity can finally be understood. To show you the difference between these two religions of Christianity and Judaism, there is a story in the book of Luke that shows the importance of Jesus' doctrine compared to the Jewish doctrine or religion. This story exposes the importance of Jesus compared to the old prophets, and it shows how Jesus would supersede the Jewish religion.

Although Jesus honored Isaiah for his contribution to God's <u>first step</u> toward_Christianity by introducing the idea that someday a special individual would come and_save the Jewish people and free them and be their king, this was Isaiah's promised Messiah and this was echoed throughout time by other prophets of the Jewish religion, and to this day they are still waiting for that promised Messiah to arrive. Naturally as a Christian, we believe he did and the Jewish leadership had him arrested and demanded his execution. It's really important to remember that the first Christians, and there were thousands, were <u>Jews.</u> (For those who don't know who Isaiah was, he was a prophet of the Jewish religion many years before Jesus was born.) That story appears in the book of Luke, chapter 4, verse 16, and it says: "And he (Jesus) came to Nazareth, where he had been brought up and as his custom was, he went into the synagogue on the Sabbath day, and stood up for to read" verse 17: "a man delivered unto him a book to read and it was the book of the prophet Isaiah. However, he did not read or quote what Isaiah wrote in the Old Testament." This appears in the book of Luke, chapter 4, verse 17: "He (Jesus) had opened from the book of Isaiah, chapter 4, verse 18, and when he had opened the book, he said, 'The spirit of the Lord is upon me, he has anointed me to preach <u>the Gospels to the poor,</u> he has sent me to heal the brokenhearted.'" But that's not what Isaiah wrote. What Isaiah wrote was "The spirit of the Lord is upon me, because the Lord hath anointed me to preach good tidings to the meek to bind up the broken-hearted." So Jesus deliberately changed the words of Isaiah in the Old Testament. Jesus went on to say "to preach deliverance to the captives." However, Isaiah wanted to free them that were in prison and seek vengeance. Jesus wanted to preach deliverance to the prisoners, not to free them. He also did not seek vengeance as Isaiah wanted. He was literally changing everything Isaiah wrote in the Old Testament. Jesus also said he was going to restore sight to the blind, something Isaiah could not do.

After Jesus completely changed the words of Isaiah, he closed the book and handed it back to the man who gave it to him. He had changed everything Isaiah wrote. He was clearly announcing to that synagogue that he was about to change everything that they believed in and he was introducing to them the Gospels. This was clearly an afront to the people in that synagogue. It ended with all of the eyes of them that were in the synagogue fastened on him. They knew exactly what Jesus had done. He had enough courage to change the words of one of the prophets, Isaiah. That's why the eyes of everyone in that synagogue were staring at him. Then he closed book and handed it to the man that gave it to him and sat down, and it says in verse 20: "And the eyes of all of them that were in the synagogue were fastened upon him." How courageous Jesus was to do this in their synagogue. But he wanted them to know that he was to supersede everything in the Old Testament. It was equivalent to a man going to the Vatican in Italy and reading from the Book of Mormon. Jesus was clearly announcing that <u>the Gospels</u> would replace the Old Testament. His words had superseded what Isaiah wrote, <u>placing himself above Isaiah</u> and informing both of the people in that synagogue and the Jewish leadership that he was their leader, their king and the promised Messiah. Jesus had the courage to read from the Old Testament and change the words of Isaiah.

How people can claim that the Bible is the Word of God after reading scriptures like this is beyond me. How many times and how many ways does Jesus have to say that we, as his followers, should only listen to him? What he read in that book of Luke, chapter 4, verse 18, was Jesus' way of explaining to the Jews that he was to supersede everything before him. Jesus never passed up the opportunity to tell the Jews that they should listen to him and not to his predecessors. He respected the old prophets, but he knew his place and he wanted them to know <u>he was their leader</u>. All Christians should know that they should accept him as their teacher and that all the Jews should listen to only him and to no one else. That he was their Messiah, not Moses or anyone else. This also applies to his own cousin, John the Baptist, who was the greatest prophet of the old law, according to Jesus the Christ. Even John the Baptist, in the book of the Apostle John, recognized Jesus and his doctrine, called Christianity, or the Kingdom of heaven, would eventually supersede him (John the Baptist) and the Jewish religion, which John the Baptist himself was part of.

In the book of John, chapter 3, verse 26, it says: "And they (the Jews that were followers of John the Baptist) came unto John and said unto him, 'Rabbi, he (Jesus) that was with thee beyond Jordan, to whom thou barest witness, behold, the same <u>baptized, and all men come to him</u>'" (implying that Jesus was becoming more popular than his cousin John the Baptist). Verse 27: "John the Baptist answered and said, 'A man can receive nothing, except <u>it be given him from heaven</u>,'" acknowledging Jesus was doing the same thing he was doing, with God's approval. In verse 28, John says: "You yourselves bear me witness that I said I am not the Christ, but that I am sent before him." Verse 29: "He that hath the bride (Jesus is the bridegroom) the friend of the bridegroom (who is <u>John the Baptist</u>) which standeth and heareth him, rejoiced greatly because of the bridegroom's voice." John the Baptist was very glad to hear his first cousin's teachings and goes on to say: "<u>This my joy therefore is fulfilled</u>" (acknowledging that he was happy to hear his cousin Jesus' doctrine), then John the Baptist goes on to say Moses doctrine' or Judaism was going to be superseded <u>by Jesus' doctrine</u> of Christianity. Verse 30: "<u>He</u> (Jesus) <u>must increase,</u>" because Jesus was preaching Christianity and John the Baptist was still preaching Judaism. But, being a Jewish prophet, <u>John says: "I must decrease,"</u> acknowledging that Christianity was going to supersede Judaism of Moses. Why? Because John the Baptist was the last and greatest Jewish prophet, according to Jesus.

John the Baptist was clearly acknowledging that Jesus and his doctrine, which is Christianity or, as it became known, as the kingdom of heaven, would supersede everything that came before him, and that included Moses and the Jewish religion. Knowing this, how could anybody come to the conclusion that the entire Bible is the Word of God? In the book of John, chapter 11, the Jews were arguing about what they wanted to do with Jesus, because of the fame that he was receiving from some of the Jewish people. Finally a man who was the head of the Jewish church took the floor, and in verse 49 it says: "And one of them named Cai-a-phas, being the high priest that same year, said unto them, 'Ye know nothing at all'" verse 50: "'nor consider that it is expedient for us, that one man should <u>die for the people</u>, and that the whole nation perish not.'" So this man knew that Jesus was a threat to the Jewish religion and was going to supersede the Jewish church of Moses. Jesus never threatened the Jewish nation; he was only a threat to the Jewish religion and their leadership. If Jesus was, in fact, the promised Messiah or the Christ of the old religion, then Jesus would be their king and Christ, and as their leader they would also have to convert over to Christianity, which the leaders of the Jewish religion would never allow. So Jesus had to die or the Jewish religion would have to die, or even worse, Jesus would be their leader. They understood the implications of Jesus being the Christ. They would also have to convert to Christianity. It was either the Jewish church, which was based on the opinion of Moses, or Jesus and Christianity. So they were going to do <u>what they thought they needed to do to survive. Killing Jesus was the logical move</u> in order to save the Jewish religion. To this day the Jewish church does not recognize Jesus as their Messiah, nor do they recognize his first cousin, John the Baptist, as a prophet; they are still waiting for the Messiah.

Now Jesus was in the horrible position of waiting for <u>his imminent death.</u> These Scriptures should convince any openminded individual that the Bible is not the Word of God. There are two stories in the Old Testament that I feel must be told. The first story is the story of Lot. It's important to remember that this story was accepted by Moses four thousand years ago to be accepted into Moses' account in the Old Testament. The story says that a man named Lot was chosen by God to go to two communities, called Sodom and Gomorrah, to find out if any of those people that lived there deserved to be saved from God's imminent destruction. <u>As if God needed Lot to determine that</u>. The story says that Lot, while visiting these two communities, was visited by two angels and the community found out about them and went to the home of Lot and wanted (as the customs of these two communities were) to have sex with them. Lot's response was absolutely horrible and was recorded in the book of Genesis, chapter 19, verse 5: "And they called unto Lot, and said unto him, 'Where are the men which came into thee this night? Bring them

out unto us <u>that we may know them</u>.'"
Make no mistake, these people wanted to have sex with these two angels. Lot's response can only be described as horrible.

Listen to what Lot, supposedly a messenger from God, told that mob. Verse 7: "Let me I pray you, brethren, do not so wickedly." Verse 8: "Behold, <u>now I have two daughters which have not known man</u>" (meaning they were virgins), "let me I pray you bring them out unto you <u>and do to them as it is good in your eyes,</u> only unto these men do nothing, for therefore came they under the shadow of my roof." Do you really believe that God would tolerate his messenger to offer his own daughters to a mob for their sexual pleasures and even to advertise to that mob that they were virgins? People who believe that this story is correct with God in this day and age are people like David Karesh and Jim Jones and many other ministers, and they are child molesters. After all, can this be wrong if it's in <u>the Word of God</u>? <u>Or is this book really the Word of God?</u> And quite frankly, it certainly casts doubt on the decency of Moses four thousand years ago. It certainly gives people insight into the minds of men years ago as well regarding women. The end of this story gets even worse. Unable to find anybody worthy to be saved, Lot was then warned of the upcoming destruction of these two communities. He and his wife and two children were warned to leave Sodom and Gomorrah and not to look back, and they did leave but Lot's wife did look back at Sodom and Gomorrah and she was turned into a pillar of salt. Then it is recorded in the book of Genesis that his two daughters decided to get their father drunk (after all, Mom was gone) and have sex with Dad, their father.

Chapter 19, verse 31: "And the first born said unto the younger, 'Our father is old, and there is not a man in the earth to come in to us after the manner of all the earth'" (as if the destruction of these two communities destroyed the entire world). Verse 32: "Come, let us make our father drink wine and we will lie with him, that we may preserve seed of our father." Verse 33: "And they made their father drink wine that night, and the firstborn went in and lay with her father, and he perceived not when she lay down nor when she arose." Verse 34: "And it came to pass on the morrow that the firstborn said unto the younger, 'Behold, I lay yesternight with my father'" verse 35: "and they made their father drink wine that night also, and the younger arose and lay with him and he precedes not when she lay down, nor when she arose." What a strange story to be in a Bible that is considered by some to be <u>the Word of God</u>. And it ended with this: verse 36: "<u>Thus were both the daughters of Lot with child by the father</u>." How can anybody read this story and think that this would be right with God? Many ministers do. After all, <u>this can't be wrong; it's in the</u>

Bible, and isn't the Bible the Word of God? This disgusting piece of pornography has been used by David Karesh and Jim Jones and many other ministers to convince their followers to give them their children for sexual pleasures. After all, this was in the Word of God, or that's what they thought. However, if the Bible is not the Word of God, as Jesus pointed out, then this was just evil and in no way represents God's approval of this disgusting behavior. Comedians used this story in a movie. Lot had taken his wife, who was turned into a pillar of salt, and stood her up in the kitchen and used her to season his food.

There is another story in the Old Testament that warrants scrutiny as well. Examining the miracles that are recorded in the Gospels, these are normal great events that can easily be understood today. Miracles like the correction of blindness, curing of diseases, and even restoring life to a dead person, all of these events are physically possible today. However, some miracles in the Old Testament are nothing more than absolute fantasy. First, let me start out by saying scientists have considered global warming and its effects for several decades. Although they disagree on the actual effects of global warming, they all agree that the melting of the North and South poles could raise the ocean's level by as much <u>as twenty feet</u>. This would be devastating for coastal areas around the world, and countries like Bangladesh would be completely inundated. However, according to the story of Noah, it states that it rained for forty days and forty nights and somehow raised the ocean levels, not by fifteen or twenty feet but somehow raised the oceans by fifteen thousand feet or more, in order to cover the mountain ranges around the world, in forty days and forty nights? This is absolutely impossible. I'm positive that the ocean level could never be raised by that much.

There are places on this planet that literally rain constantly; they are referred to as rainforests. Furthermore, the logistical problems of getting two animals of each specie on the planet from where they are to that boat is impossible. Most of the animals would have to cross thousands of miles of ocean to get to that boat. How did the polar bears get to that boat? How did the creatures from Australia get to that boat? Kangaroos, koala bears and many other creatures are unique to Australia, along with their diets. Many other animals are unique to different parts of the world and have unique diets as well that they can only get from their own habitat. Two bears, two elephants, two giraffes, two hippopotamuses, two lions, two horses, two cats, two dogs, two gorillas, two porcupines, two cows, two kangaroos, even two rattlesnakes? I'm sure the two rats were very nervous about that addition, and consider the thousands of species of birds, including two hummingbirds and two condors. I hope you get the picture. Consider the food and water it would require to feed them and to provide for them; this task is impossible. And as one comedian asked, "<u>And who was going to clean up that mess at the bottom of the boat every day. Pee-eew</u>!" Between the weight of the animals, the food supply to feed them, and the water that would be required to provide for those animals, along with the mess at the bottom of the boat, this would sink the boat.

That story was created to impress people <u>five thousand years ago</u>. Why do I say that? There is a story that predates Moses by one thousand years. And that story is close or identical to Moses' story. Moses obviously either read that story or heard about it, and he incorporated that story into his account of the history of the world <u>that he created</u>. Welcome to the 21st century. A small humorous note: A replica of Noah's Ark was built and they found that the boat had to be covered and protected from the rain. The wood of the boat was suffering from water damage. If you're wondering how anybody could build a replica of Noah's Ark, it's because the exact measurements are recorded in the Bible. So many <u>cubits</u> by so many <u>cubits</u> are recorded in the Bible. Anybody that thinks this book called the Holy Bible, created by the Catholic Church, is in fact the Word of God and God would tolerate or condone men sleeping with their daughters and having sex with them and getting them pregnant is wrong. This type of behavior is an absolute insult to our Father in heaven. Furthermore, the story of Noah is scientifically impossible. It's stories like these that will discourage young people from believing in the Holy Bible, because today's society would never tolerate such behavior as the story about Lot sleeping with his daughters and getting them pregnant (this story should be in a <u>porno bookstore</u>), not <u>the Holy Bible</u>. How could anybody believe this story could possibly be morally correct? As for the story of Noah, who somehow saved the entire world in a canoe, it's absurd. This should take us to another subject: Is there any scientific evidence that proves God exists?

Chapter Three
The Scientific Evidence of God

How and when was the universe created? The answer is 13.7 <u>billion</u> years ago the universe came into existence, with something that is referred to as <u>the Big Bang</u>; however, as scientists pointed out, it was neither big nor was there an audible sound of *bang*. According to scientists, the universe started out being no larger than a blood cell in your body. With the creation of the universe came the first indication of a God. Why? Because for some unknown reason, a source of <u>energy</u> was created with it. Without this energy, the universe would have been a complete void of nothing. Where it came from, nobody has any idea. This energy created every single solitary thing in our universe. Every planet, moon, asteroid, comet, and sun, indeed every single solitary thing that is matter came from this source of energy. Scientists have absolutely no idea where this energy came from. This miracle has led many scientists to believe that there must, in fact, be a God. Where it came from, God only knows.

For thousands of years, men have looked at the heavens and wondered, what is this thing? The answer to this question began in the 1500s. There was a little boy who stared at the heavens every <u>cloudless</u> night and carefully plotted the location of all the glowing objects that were visible. His name was Tycho. Tycho did this for many years and made a discovery that he could not understand. After decades of doing this, and unable to understand what he was observing, he went to the Catholic Church because he knew that Catholic priests were also looking at the heavens and asked them if they knew anybody that could solve some unusual observation that he discovered. The Catholic Church introduced him to a little boy, thirteen years of age, saying this little boy, Johan Kepler, was a genius and he could solve any problem. So he hired this young boy in hopes that Johan

Kepler could help him understand what he was observing in the evening skies. Tycho hoped that by talking to young Kepler, he might be able to solve these unusual observation that he discovered. His discovery was that he viewed five objects in the evening skies that were doing something he could not understand. Two of these objects that he viewed seemed to be in a race with each other. One of them would always outrace the other, and this was occurring more than once each year and three other objects were doing something even more strange. They were appearing periodically (not every year) in the heavens, but they were doing something that he could not understand. They would travel across the skies periodically in a straight line for a while, and for some unknown reason they would stop moving forward and then they would go backwards for a short period of time and then stop again and continue moving forwards once more. What would make an object travel forward, then stop, then travel backwards and stop again and then continue moving forward again?

Tycho and Johan Kepler talked about Tycho's observations for years and discussed all of the possibilities of what these objects were doing and why. Young Kepler kept asking Tycho if he could see all of his data that he had collected throughout the years, but Tycho refused. He did not want Kepler to see all of his information that he had gathered, because he wanted to take all of the credit of solving this mystery of what was going on. Years went by without them discovering what Tycho had uncovered. Finally, Tycho died. This put Kepler, now a full-grown man, in the position of convincing Tycho's widow to allow him to see all of Tycho's work. He promised her that if he ever solved the mystery of what these objects were doing, and why they were doing it, he would give her deceased husband the credit he deserved for accumulating this information and she agreed. And since I know Tycho's name, he obviously kept his word. After years of reviewing all of Tycho's work, he finally discovered that for some unknown reason, to Kepler these five objects, along with the planet Earth, were for some reason in an elliptical orbit around the sun. He was correct. These objects turned out to be five planets, and they were named Mercury and Venus, which were closer to the sun than Earth was, and Mars, Jupiter and Saturn, which were farther away from the sun than Earth was. However, why they were in elliptical orbits around the sun would remain a mystery for almost two hundred years.

That's when in the 1700s, a man named Isaac Newton discovered why they were in elliptical orbit around the sun. He would be the man that discovered that there was a force in the universe called gravity, which explained why Earth and these other objects were in elliptical orbit around the sun. All of these things would be called a solar system, and as telescopes improved three other objects were also discovered in elliptical orbit around the sun and would be added to our solar system, which were the planets Uranus, Neptune, and Pluto. Now a small piece of the universe was understood. Two hundred years later, Albert Einstein showed up and gave us even more information about the universe. An interesting note is Johan Kepler, Isaac Newton, and Albert Einstein all believed in God. This brings us to a particular scientific law regarding the universe that is profound and unexplained and has led many scientists to believe that there <u>must be a God</u>. Everything in the universe is either matter (which is everything solid) or energy like electricity.

Now listen carefully to this law. This law states that neither <u>energy like electricity nor matter</u>, which is everything solid in our universe, can neither be <u>created nor destroyed</u>; you can only change one of these two things into the other. This is a puzzle and a paradox <u>*that exists in our universe*</u>. The puzzle or paradox is if energy or matter <u>cannot be created or destroyed</u> but can only be changed from one of these things into the other, what are these two things doing here and where did they come from? This is what scientists have to accept. The truth is that everything in the universe is impossible to be here, because everything in the universe is either matter or energy and neither one of these things can be created or destroyed and yet both are here. This is why the greatest scientists in the world believe in God. So if the greatest scientists in the world can believe in God, and many do, people like you and me can also. So, if you believe in God, you are in good company.

When the universe began, somehow energy came with it and nobody knows why. Without this energy the universe would be a complete void of nothing. So where did it come from? There is absolutely no scientific or logical reason for this to have happened. Now the question is, is it possible that the energy that magically came with the universe could possibly make matter? Some scientists questioned the possibility that energy could, in fact, make matter. Can you make something solid out of electricity? Everything in the universe is either matter, which is everything solid, such as planets, asteroids, moons, meteors, comets and suns, indeed everything physical or solid that exists in the universe, and the other is energy such as light, electricity, x-rays, gamma rays and all forms of energy. These two things make up the entire universe. However, the law in our universe says that neither matter nor energy can be <u>created</u> or <u>destroyed</u> and scientists are forced to accept this law or reality. Again this law states that neither matter (everything physical) nor energy (which is everything else in our universe) can be created or destroyed, but both can only be changed from one into the another. Now the question is, since we know energy came with the creation of the universe, can energy create matter? Many scientists doubted that energy like lightning or electricity could create matter, something solid. It's easy to understand how matter can create energy because a simple example of this part of the law is if you place a piece of wood on a burning fire, that wood would be turned into energy. You can physically feel the energy by the heat it creates, but can energy create matter? Many scientists doubted that energy (such as electricity, x-rays and gamma rays or other forms of energy) could possibly make matter. However, this was proven decades ago when scientists built a giant seventeen-mile circular tunnel called the Colider, where they created matter by forcing energy, propelled at high speeds, in opposite directions, causing the energy to collide together. After years of doing this, some energy <u>was, in fact</u>, converted into a piece of matter, proving that one can be converted into the other and proving that they are the same exact thing but in different forms. So if energy and matter are the same thing and are interchangeable and neither one can be created or destroyed, the question must be asked, where did the energy come from? This is something that has baffled scientists since it was discovered. It's like, what came first, the chicken or the egg? <u>This is why many scientists believe in God</u>. The scientists who did speculate the possibility that energy could, in fact, create matter, decades before it was proven, called this first particle of matter that would or could be created <u>the God particle</u>. This process of energy making matter went on for millions or billions of years, making everything solid in our universe. Many scientists believe in God, even though they do not attend an organized religious church.

Some scientists did not believe that energy could create matter, but it happened. So now we know how the planets, moons, comets, asteroids, suns and everything solid in our universe came about. Now this brings us to the next gigantic question.

CHAPTER FOUR
GOD'S CREATION OF LIFE

How did life get started or created on planet Earth? This question would seem to be impossible to answer; however, it can be logically figured out. So hang in there with me and I'll try to explain it as simply and as clearly as I can.

How can a living organism on planet Earth be created? The first step of creating a living creature is the collection and assembly of something called amino acids. These are the building blocks of cells, of all living things, and are much, much smaller than the cell itself. Amino acids are the building block of cells and cells are the things that make up all living organisms. These amino acids made the first cells of the first living creature on earth. Since amino acids make up the cells in <u>all living organisms,</u> whether it be a plant or an animal, it would certainly take thousands of these extremely tiny amino acids to make the first living cells of an organism on planet Earth. This is the first strange and bizarre coincidence that occurred. Amino acids come in two different and opposite forms. They are either <u>righthanded</u> or <u>lefthanded</u> and should have been evenly available and <u>evenly used</u>; however, they were not. Living organisms have a very unusual percentage of these two types of amino acids. Instead of having a 50-50 percentage of these two types of amino acids, <u>righthanded amino acids</u> far outnumber lefthanded amino acids, and scientists do not know why. It was as if <u>they were selected</u> rather than randomly chosen, and <u>God only knows why</u>. There were many more righthanded amino acids used, compared to the lefthanded amino acids. This defies logic. It was like the hand of God reached into this giant bowl of soup and <u>selected,</u> rather than randomly chosen, to create this first living organism. This is astounding and incredible and <u>scientists have absolutely no idea why this occurred</u>. The creature it created millions of years ago becomes a <u>much more compli-</u>

cated organism. (Please be patient with me as I try to explain the following steps that had to occur for this first creature (that is not alive yet) to continue its process of becoming a living organism.)

The next <u>nine steps had to happen in order for this first creature to fulfill its apparent mission, of creating all life on Earth.</u> How did life get started or get <u>created?</u> Was it <u>natural</u> or did God create life? <u>You decide.</u>

Step #1: The amino acids had to be <u>selected</u> and assembled in_the proper and perfect order in order to create the cells of this first living organism, whether it was an animal or a plant. Keep in mind that all living creatures, whether they be animal or plant, have to accomplish these things (so now it is a_creature, <u>but it isn't alive yet</u>).

Step #2: It had to receive <u>an electrical charge</u> in order to start living. Why? For the same reason that when a person stops breathing and dies, they require a medical procedure of an electrical charge to revive them. This would also apply to that first creature; however, this first creature had an additional problem to overcome.

Step #3: If the electrical charge that was used to bring it alive was too strong, this first creature could have been damaged beyond repair, or if the electrical charge was too weak it might not have been affective, so it had to have the absolute correct electrical charge and it obviously got it.

(<u>It's alive</u>, —-- I was sure God knew what he was doing.)

Step #4: Stimulating this first, <u>now living</u> creature, this electoral charge <u>had to be very soon</u> after its creation. Why? Because anything dead, <u>and it was</u>, begins to deteriorate. You could not revive a dead person hours after that person dies *<u>unless you were God</u>*.

Now the next two steps are imperative. Step #5: It required something to eat, all living creature do, whether it be a plant or an animal; and Step #6: It also required the ability to consume that food source. All creatures require this as well (I hope I haven't lost you yet. Hang in there, we are almost done.) because everything alive requires these two things no matter if it is a plant or animal. So these two things needed to be available and apparently they were. To explain how necessary these two things are, if there was no food available, it would've died and if the food source was available to consume and it had no way of consuming it, it would also die. Again, this also applies if it was a plant or animal. These two things were absolutely important and <u>imperative</u>.

The next step was Step #7: There had to be a way of processing the food it ate. Again, all living creatures require this, both animals and plants. This required a digestive system of some sort. All living things do, no matter if it is grass in your front yard or a vegetable plant, or a tree or a mosquito or any other living organism. Step #8: It would also require a way of eliminating some things that it consumed or it doesn't need; both animals and plants do this. Because if it didn't eliminate some things it consumed, and all things do, it would just get larger and larger until it exploded. Thank God plants don't like oxygen, because we need that. Another thing to consider: Was the first creature <u>an animal and it created a plant,</u> or was the first living creature a plant and it created an animal, or were they both created separately at the same time, or individually at different times? (Wow, that's something to consider.) Could this have come about without God's guidance?

Now Step #9: This next step of this first living creature, and the following one, is in my opinion absolutely impossible <u>without the assistance and guidance of a divine individual</u>. This is where me and scientists who believe in <u>natural evolution</u> do not agree. In order to explain how life continued on the planet, they assumed that this first living organism had the ability to either <u>clone itself</u> or <u>duplicate itself</u>, but this could not have occurred. Why? Because if it duplicated or cloned itself, it would have been identical in <u>size, shape, color and age.</u> This, in fact, was the greatest and most crucial and important accomplishment that could have ever occurred without the aid <u>of a divine individual</u>. Why? Because no matter how many times it duplicated or cloned itself, its duplicate or clone would all be the <u>same shape</u>, the <u>same</u>

size, and the <u>same color</u> and unfortunately <u>the same age,</u> and if that was true, they would all die together. So the scientists must be wrong.

Step #9: This first living creature did not clone or duplicate itself; it cloned or duplicated itself, <u>in a younger version of itself;</u> it was <u>asexual</u> (a creature that could impregnate itself). <u>It</u> <u>literally had a baby.</u> This also applies to plant life, because nothing lives forever. That, my friends, had to be <u>planned and designed,</u> and anything that is planned or designed requires a <u>planner or a designer.</u> There is no other explanation for this to have occur. It also did something even more impossible than having a baby.

Step #10: Its <u>DNA was eventually changed and</u> somehow altered into another type of living organism successfully, and this also applies to either a plant or an animal. Do you have any idea how difficult changing the DNA is? This had to be the greatest accomplishment that could ever have occurred without God's assistance. Whatever it changed into, that creature also changed its DNA and was changed into another creature as well, and this went on for millions of years into every living thing that has lived on this planet, no matter if it was an animal or a plant. The DNA was changed into every microorganism, every pre-dinosaur, every dinosaur, or every single solitary plant—indeed, every single solitary living creature that has ever existed on Earth came from something previous by altering its DNA. These ten steps had to be accomplished in order to make all life-forms on planet Earth. Something happened along the way that was absolutely incredible as well. Some animals changed from <u>asexual</u> (the ability to reproduce itself in a younger form, without a mate) to sexual (in order to reproduce, it required both a male and a female. This transitional change was astounding.), and this change some created emotionally. They eventually acquired the need of companionship; if it were an animal, it began to care, and millions of years later this would evolve to love. You may call this natural evolution but I call it one miracle after another, <u>and all without God's assistance?</u> I don't think that's possible, do you? Each time a new organism came into existence, no matter if it was an animal or a plant, its DNA required changing. And obviously this happened millions of times over and over again. The different organisms on this planet, no matter if it were an animal or a plant, required its DNA to be changed or altered over and over again successfully for millions of years. Every creature or plant life has a different DNA, which means that the DNA has been altered literally millions of times <u>successfully</u>.

In my humble opinion, this could've never happened without the assistance and guidance of God. This has to be considered a miracle. Humans with our technology have altered the DNA, by our own technology. We did it accidentally and it has never been beneficial. Why? <u>Changing the DNA</u> of any creature has always been detrimental. X-rays and gamma rays have been able to change the DNA of living creatures and, without exception, have hurt or damaged the living organism; however, the DNA of every organism that followed was changed or altered successfully. When the DNA is altered by us it's overwhelmingly dangerous and harmful. To give you a good example of the problems of changing the DNA successfully, it was in the 1950s. Some men were exposing rose plants to radiation and it changed the DNA of a rose plants, and scientists were able to create a new type of rose plant. <u>The Queen Elizabeth rose plant</u>. It was more beautiful <u>to us</u> than other rose plants, and it was hailed a great success. However, it turned out that it was a weaker plant and it required more water and more attention to keep it alive. Although it was a much more beautiful rose plant <u>to us</u>, it was damaged in some way.

To explain how difficult it is to alter DNA successfully, when America dropped an atomic bomb on Hiroshima in Japan and, a few days later, dropped another bomb on the city of Nagasaki in 1945, it altered the DNA of many humans and, I imagine, plants as well around the world, and nothing beneficial came from it. It was always detrimental. No matter how many times the DNA was changed, <u>it was, in fact, always and without excep-</u>

tion detrimental and destructive, and yet the DNA from that first creature on earth was changed successfully millions of times. Every other organism that came into existence was changed successfully as well, and it happened over and over and over again, millions of times, successfully. Some creatures' DNA were changed from asexual, not requiring a mate, to sexual, requiring a mate. This required a gigantic alteration of the DNA. For me this is proof that God exists.

Two hundred thousand years ago, the DNA of one animal was changed and another creature came into existence. It was a human being. What creature's DNA was altered to bring us into existence? Scientist have speculated <u>that this creature must have been a gorilla.</u> Why? Because a gorilla has 98 percent of a human's DNA, and this change was so successful that we lost most of our hair and entered into a cave for protection from the elements, learned how to create and use fire, grow and harvest food, invented the wheel, organized and created empires, manufactured automobiles, created weapons powerful enough to destroy the entire world, and went to the moon. If 2 percent of the gorilla DNA made us what we are, what would happen if 2 percent of our DNA was changed? Could we become gods ourselves? Gorillas, on the other hand, have accomplished absolutely nothing. <u>Are we not God's greatest accomplishment?</u> Could this have been accomplished without our heavenly Father? And what do we owe him, <u>besides everything?</u> How much has a gorilla accomplished in that same period of time? He's still meandering through the jungle looking for food or he's in a cage in the zoo. <u>God is great</u>.

When men or human beings change the DNA of any living creature, it has been overwhelmingly harmful and yet, from the beginning of life on planet Earth, living creatures' DNA, including plants, were changed over and over and over again *successfully*. This would seem to defy logic. <u>But God did it</u>. For these reasons, I truly believe that evolution of species has to be a <u>controlled and a guided process. You must know ex-</u>

actly how to do it, or it will be dangerous and harmful. Just randomly
changing the DNA will always be
negative. If you ever alter the DNA,
you must be able to understand exactly how to do it; otherwise, it will be
disastrous and harmful because it requires intelligent guidance.

There was a study of a fossil record
years ago. Scientists studied a particular fossil record near an island that had
an unbroken and complete record of
many sea creatures that came into existence. This fossil record was the
most complete fossil record that has
ever been found on this planet, and it
recorded many living creatures, cov-
ering a timespan of sixty million years
of lifeforms, that came into existence
and then went extinct millions of

years later. Now scientists had a first-time opportunity to view and study sixty million years of lifeforms and <u>made a startling discovery</u>. This unbroken record revealed that every creature that came into existence in that particular area and then eventually went extinct could only accomplish two things during each specie's existence. Each organism appeared in the fossil record fully formed but miniature in size and could only change their physical size and their physical color. This is all each organism did in that unbroken fossil record of <u>sixty million years</u>. They appeared <u>fully developed but extremely small in size and could only change their physical color and their physical size. This is all those creatures did or could do be-</u>

fore they went extinct. They never saw one creature slowly evolving into another, and this came from the most complete intact fossil record ever discovered on planet Earth. Unlike other scientific evolutionary studies, which concluded evolution happened over a long period of time, with small changes. This did not occur in that sixty-million-year period in that part of the world. When the scientists studied that sixty-million-year record, they expected to see one creature slowly evolving or changing into another; however, without exception each specie that came into existence in that sixty-million-year period always appeared in a miniature form, and the only changes that occurred were their physical size and their physical color during their existence. <u>Without ex-</u><u>ception</u>, this is all those species did, and then they went extinct. There was no slow evolving from one creature into another. This form of evolution was called <u>punctuated equilibrium</u>. There was no specie <u>in that sixty-mil-</u><u>lion-year period</u>, in that record and in that part of the ocean, that ever evolved into another creature and then <u>they would go extinct.</u>

It's good to remember that this fossil record is the best and unbroken record of lifeforms that exist on this planet <u>to this day</u>. All other fossil records are much less complete. <u>Punctuated equilibrium</u> is, in fact, the most complete and unbroken record of fossils on this planet. Is it possible that they were not looking at evolution; <u>they were observing creation?</u> Many species today can be described in the same way. Horses are different sizes and different colors, so are dogs and so are cats, even people can be described the same way, of different sizes and different colors. So where is this evidence of creatures evolving slowly from one creature into another? <u>It doesn't exist.</u> All other studies of evolution are not as complete because they are based upon much shorter periods of time for their evidence. Their fossil records show some creatures resembling others, but there isn't a clear or complete record of one specie ever evolving slowly into another.

So, allow me to review those ten steps that had to be made to create the first living creature.

When God created the first living organism, these are the steps that the first and other living organism accomplished to create a world of life. #1: It used two different forms of the amino acids. Although they were both equally available, righthanded amino acids seemed to be preferred for some reason, more than lefthanded amino acids, suggesting that they were chosen or selected to be used disproportionately. #2: It required many thousands of these building blocks to create the first living cell or creature. #3: There was a perfect arrangement of them to create the first living organism. #4: The perfect electrical charge to stimulate it into life. #5: These four steps had to occur within a very short period of time of this organism's creation. #6: It required food, which was obviously available. #7: It required the ability to consume the available food source. #8: It could give birth to a younger version of itself, <u>meaning it had a baby and eventually went from asexual to sexual.</u> #9: Each new creature that came into existence had a different DNA. #10: This process went on for millions of years successfully and created every other living organism, which included every plant, whether it be grass, vegetable, plant, or a tree, indeed every living thing on this planet, by its DNA being altered successfully. This first organism literally made it possible to create a planet of living creatures.

When you consider all the things that each individual organism had to accomplish by altering its DNA, <u>which humans</u> are unable to do today successfully, but <u>nature or God</u> did, this must be considered a miracle. Do you believe that any of this could've come about without a deity's guidance? The only thing that is obvious <u>to me</u> is—<u>GOD IS GREAT!</u>

CHAPTER FIVE
THE SCIENTIFIC EVIDENCE OF THE SHROUD OF TURIN

For nonbelievers of God, here is something else to consider: When God's son (Jesus) was executed, some people placed his body on a piece of cloth that covered his entire torso, from his head all the way down to his feet and all the way up his back, to his head. This is referred to as a burial cloth or a shroud and is known today as the Shroud of Turin because that is where it is located, in Italy. Three days after the Jews and the Romans killed Jesus the "Christ," or the son of God, a woman named Mary Magdalena went to his tomb and discovered that it was empty; however, the shroud of Jesus that covered his body was still there. This story is recorded in the Bible.

Another story in another book says Mary Magdalena took the shroud to the wife of Pontius Pilate, the judge at Jesus' trial, and showed it to her. The story says that Pilate's wife gave it to Luke, one of the men who wrote one of the Gospels in the Holy Bible, and Luke gave it to a man named Thaddeus, who took it to a king in Turkey. That king's name was King Abgar. Why did he take the shroud to Turkey? First, to get it out of Jerusalem and protect it from the Jewish leadership hands for safekeeping, and second, because Jesus wanted to help a king in Turkey because this king had leprosy and requested Jesus to come and heal him. According to the story, Jesus sent him a message saying that he could not come; however, he would send him something that would help him. What that something was, was Jesus' burial shroud. When the man delivered the shroud to the king in Turkey, a light emulated from the shroud and filled the entire room and that light cured the king and his righthand man, who made paganistic head dressings for the king, who also had leprosy. The king was so grateful that he and his right-hand man converted to Christianity.

Years later, someone made the king a medallion that reflected the king's face on one side and the face of Jesus on the other side. On that medallion on the face of Jesus, there appears an odd-shaped square. This odd-shaped square on Jesus' cheek has no artistic or religious value; it's just a blemish on the material of the shroud. This medallion would positively prove two thousand years later that the carbon dating of the shroud two thousand years later was incorrect. Why? Because whoever created that medallion for the king placed an odd-shaped square on the face of Jesus. Why is this so important? Because that mark on Jesus' face on the shroud has no artistic or religious value; it is just a blemish <u>on the material of the cloth of the shroud.</u> This blemish on the face of Jesus appears on many paintings and drawings and frescoes throughout Europe that other artists created of the images of Jesus. So, the medallion of King Abgar is proof that in the first century somebody was looking at the shroud, proving that the carbon-14 dating of the shroud two thousand years later was, in fact, incorrect.

When King Abgar died, his first son took his place and continued following the religion of Christianity. However, when his first son died, his second son took the first son's place as king and he wanted to return to the paganistic religion that his father believed in before he converted to Christianity. He sent his guards to the home of King Abgar's righthand man's home and ordered him to return to the castle and start making paganistic head dressings for him. King Abgar's righthand man refused because he had become a Christian minister. The second son, who became king, was angered and told his guards to go back to the righthand man's home and break his legs as punishment, which they did. This unfortunately would soon cause his death. However, before he died, he requested his Christian followers to hide the shroud and the medallion. They took the shroud and the medallion with the odd-shaped square on Jesus' face and hid it in the wall that surrounded the city, and this is where it remained for the next five hundred years.

In the year 525, there was a massive flood in Turkey and there was a great amount of damage to the city and to the wall that surrounded it. This story is important because it will verify the authenticity of the burial cloth of Christ and prove that the carbon dating of the shroud two thousand years later was wrong and also proof that Jesus was the son of God and proving that God exists. Why? Because that blemish of that <u>odd-shaped square on the face of Jesus,</u> on the burial cloth of Christ, appears on the medallion of King Abgar. This mark or blemish is not part of the image; it is just a blemish on the material of the shroud, caused by the way it was folded. This blemish on the right cheek of the image of Jesus appears on that medallion of King Abgar, proving that it existed during King Abgar's reign shortly after the time of Jesus' execution and completely discredits the findings of the carbon-14 dating of the burial shroud of Jesus Christ two thousand years later.

From the time the shroud was uncovered from the wall surrounding the city in Turkey in the year of 525, the shroud was transferred many times to one location after another and from one group of people to another. It eventually arrived at St. John the Baptist Cathedral, located in Turin, Italy, where it remains to this day and is referred to as <u>the Shroud of Turin</u>. However, before it arrived there, it was first publicly displayed years earlier in France in the year 1357 and was being displayed <u>as a likeness</u> of Jesus Christ, but privately they were declaring it as the actual burial cloth of Jesus Christ. On this piece of material was a complete image of a man who resembled an individual who had experienced everything that Christ endured during his crucifixion. "Almost" everything that happened to Jesus during his execution, according to the Bible, is displayed on this piece of cloth. The image on that piece of material reflected the wounds that Jesus endured, according to the Bible, with one exception, the location of the spikes driven through the hands, and this was proven that the shroud was correct and the Bible's account was wrong. This piece of cloth was three feet wide and fourteen feet long and displayed a full image of a man from his head down to his feet and from the bottom of the feet all the way up the back of his body to his head. A full image of an apparently crucified individual. This burial cloth changed hands numerous times and in numerous locations and eventually was stored in St. John the Baptist's chapel, located in Turin, Italy, where it remains to this day.

Many people, including the Vatican Church, thought that this was actually the burial cloth of Jesus and it showed the crucified image of Jesus Christ, although the Vatican never officially recognized it as the burial cloth of Jesus Christ. This piece of material has been owned, protected and stored by the Vatican until today. The debate over its authenticity had gone on for over six hundred years.

Many people were convinced that it was a 14th-century European painting or some sort of artistic endeavor and a forgery, while others believed it was the actual burial cloth of Jesus the Christ. In 1978 the Catholic Church invited scientists from all over the world to examine this cloth and hopefully solve the mystery once and for all. Was it a painting, a drawing, or was it a miracle? A total of 120 hours were allocated to the scientists to solve the mystery. One hundred twenty hours to use everything that was available that could determine what made this image. The only restriction was they could not physically touch it.

There were some scientists that were convinced it was a European forgery and others, not so sure. Even before going to Turin, Italy, there was some data already gathered about the shroud. The first scientific data came in 1902 by using a relatively new invention called a camera. A man named Seconda Pia, who had some awards using this relatively new device, was called upon to photograph the cloth for a historic record because the image on the shroud is fading away. When he arrived at the church, he set up his camera and lights and photographed the shroud and took his work back to his lab to develop the film, and when he did, much to his shock the image on the <u>negative</u> was a <u>positive,</u> which meant the body of Jesus image was a positive and the image on the shroud was a negative. So he took the picture of the shroud, which he expected would be a negative and would require developing, but his negative was a positive. The implication was obvious to a photographer, the image on the shroud was a negative, that emulated from the body of Jesus, which was a positive. This would make sense if the energy that made the image on the shroud emulated from the body of Jesus, which was a positive, when he was resurrected and brought back to life. This convinced Seconda Pia that it was authentic.

About two decades later, a French doctor tried to reproduce the crucifixion of Jesus according to the Bible by using a cadaver and discovered that a spike driven through the palms of the hands, as the Bible claimed, could not support the weight of a human body. The human hand does not have sufficient bone structure to support the weight of a human. Every time he tried to crucify a dead body, the spike ripped through the hands, and the body would fall off the cross. It was clear that the Bible's account of Jesus' crucifixion was wrong. Abandoning the Bible's account of the crucifixion, he examined the image on the shroud and realized that the spikes were not located in the palms of his hands, as the Bible stated, but were driven through the wrists. By crucifying cadavers in the same manner that was displayed on the shroud, he discovered that by driving the spike through the <u>wrist,</u> there was sufficient bone structure to support the weight of the human body and, at the same time, solved a mystery regarding the image on the shroud. The mystery on the shroud was, <u>where are Jesus' thumbs?</u> They are not visible on the shroud; only his four fingers on each hand are visible. When he drove the spikes through the wrists of the cadaver, as it appears <u>on the shroud</u>, he discovered that it not only could support the weight of the body; it also <u>convulsed the thumbs</u> into the palms of the hands, and by driving the spikes through the wrists it also pinched a nerve that runs up the arms and into the chest, preventing the victim's ability to breathe. The fact that the spike was in the wrists, rather than the palms of his hands, as the Bible states, is the reason the Catholic Church or

Vatican had been reluctant to formally accept it as authentic.

The Bible was wrong and was proven wrong scientifically. It also explains what causes humans to die when they are crucified. When the nerve is pinched in the wrist, that nerve runs up a person's arm and cramps the lungs and the person is unable to breathe. So the crucified victim, in order to breathe, must stand or raise himself by using the spike driven through his feet. This allows the victim to relieve the pressure of the median nerve and he is able to breathe; however, you can't stand on that spike forever and you collapse. It is a slow and agonizing death. Standing on the spike driven through the feet, allowing you to breathe and then collapsing and preventing you from breathing, and you begin to suffocate. The Roman Empire, who invented this horrible form of execution, had a mercy procedure. If the victim was still alive after six hours of torture, they would mercifully end their agony by breaking the victim's legs so they could no longer stand on the spike and you would immediately die by suffocation. This is how Jesus, our beloved Savior, died.

Also about the same time the French scientist was making his discovery regarding crucifixions, another scientist in 1920 postulated that _if_ the shroud was, in fact, the burial cloth of Jesus and the energy that made the image on the shroud emulated from Jesus' body. As photographer Segunda

Pia discovered, when he was brought back to life there would be a shroud body distance factor. What that meant is, the material of the shroud would rest on Jesus' forehead and on his nose and on his chin and on his chest, but not the recesses of his eyes, the recesses of the bottom of his nose and his lips, and would rest on his chin and on his chest, but not the recesses of his neck. These parts of Jesus' body would be slightly farther away from the material of the cloth.

So the forehead, the nose, the chin and the chest would be minutely brighter than the recesses of the other parts of his body, the recesses of his eyes, the bottom of his nose and his lips, and the recesses of his neck would be farther away from the cloth and minutely less bright. However, in 1920 there was no way of proving this theory. But in 1978, when the Vatican was ready to allow the scientists to examine the shroud, there was a way of proving this theory. Dr. Jackson, the head of the American portion of the Turin Commission, remembered reading about the scientist who postulated this theory of the shroud body distant factor, and he realized there was <u>possibly</u> a way he could prove this theory. There was a space-age instrument called a VP8 analyzer. This instrument could accurately determine how far a particular star was from Earth. The star that it was used on was a star known as a Cepheid Variable. This type of star periodically increases in luminosity over a period of time and always reaches a particular brightness and when it does, this instrument can determine the exact distance it is from Earth. Then the star reduces in luminosity. This instrument can determine how far this type of star is, even though it is millions of light years away from Earth. It is extremely sensitive that it can count the rays of light or photons to make the calculation of the distance, from that star to the earth.

To explain the sensitivity of this apparatus, a photograph of two men holding a 1000-watt bulb many miles away from this apparatus, this device could accurately determine the exact distance these bulbs are from the VP8 analyzer. It's that sensitive. Dr. Jackson wondered what the VP8 analyzer would make of the image on the shroud. Could it determine <u>the points of contact</u> the shroud made with Jesus' face? Would there, in fact, be a shroud body distance factor as the scientist in 1920 predicted? The only photograph Dr. Jackson could get of the shroud was a 1935 picture of it, so he fed the photograph into the VP8 analyzer and, much to his surprise and the entire world, it produced a three-dimensional image of the face of Jesus that was on the shroud. The shroud body distance factor, postulated in 1920 by a scientist, was, in fact, <u>real</u>. The forehead, nose, chin and chest were protruded and the eyes, mouth and neck were recessed; the image on the shroud was a three-dimensional image. The photo made headlines all around the world and people were praising the shroud as the burial cloth of Jesus Christ. Dr. Jackson was convinced even before he went to Italy that the shroud was authentic. Now interest in examining this piece of material up close took on renewed enthusiasm. The men and women that would participate in the examination of the shroud had to raise their own revenue to get to the shroud in Turin, Italy. So loans had to be made on their homes, boats were sold and each person had to raise money to finance their own transportation, and also a lot of equipment had to be purchased and passports had to be acquired. The problems seemed to be monumental but one by one each obstacle was overcome.

Then came the acquisition and the transportation of the special electronic instrument needed to investigate the shroud, and no less than eight tons of equipment in all had to be transported to Italy. The Italian customs service also presented additional obstacles that had to be addressed and overcome, but with determination, tenacity and <u>a little luck,</u> the Turin Commission prevailed. One hundred twenty hours seemed generous at first; however, there were four hundred scientists from all over the world that wanted to be part of the investigation, and it made this one hundred twenty hours of time seem inadequate. They had so much to accomplish within that time period that they wondered if they could accomplish it all. Not only American scientists were interested in this piece of cloth but other countries from all over the world were as well.

So once the scientists arrived and began collecting their scientific data, as one group of scientists completed their investigation, another group was waiting, and other scientists would help them set up their equipment for their investigation. The cooperation between different groups of scientists was amazing. When one group finished their investigation, they would quickly remove their equipment and assisted the next group of scientists to set up their equipment. To completely comprehend the thoroughness of their research, thirty thousand photographs were taken of the shroud. Although touching the shroud was forbidden, the cameras could get within a thousandth of an inch from it. One of the first things they wanted to investigate was, is this image a painting or drawing? What they looked for were brush marks. Was it a painting? If it was, it would not only have brush marks, but it would also show signs of capillarity. Capillarity is how liquid such as water, oil, or any fluid gets absorbed into a porous surface, and also, if any earth pigments were used. What was the image made of?

Finally, the question was going to be answered: Did an artist do this? The answer was, there were no brush marks, no capillarity and no earth pigments. The image seemed to be literally burned into the material of the shroud and in a three-dimensional form, just as predicted in 1920 by the scientist who stated <u>there would be a shroud body distance factor.</u> While all the data or information was being collected, <u>a new member</u> was being added to the investigation. The man's name was Dr. Max Freid. Dr. Freid was a photographic expert and, more importantly, <u>a botanist</u> (an expert on plants). The addition of this man to the investigating team could easily be interpreted as <u>a gift from God</u>, and he was a criminologist. He was <u>an open skeptic regarding the shroud's authenticity</u>. His job or responsibility was to examine each photograph that was taken of the shroud for any signs of manipulation or any tampering of each photo.

While examining each photograph taken of the shroud, he noticed that each photo up close had what looked like dust particles <u>in</u> the material. Since he was a detective by trade, he wondered what these particles were. Remember, this cloth was thought to be, by many skeptics, a 14th-century European forgery because it was first publicly displayed in France in Europe. He approached the authorities of the Vatican and requested permission to remove these particles to examine them under a high-powered microscope. Since nobody was allowed to touch the shroud, by the Vatican, he convinced them that he could accomplish the removal of these particles without touching the shroud physically. How was this going to be accomplished? By placing a wide piece of adhesive tape onto the cloth, without touching it, then pressing down on it with a roller and removing the tape carefully, all without touching the cloth. The Vatican consented with the condition that this procedure would be carefully supervised.

When he removed these particles from inside the shroud, he took them back to a laboratory and examined each of these particles, and it revealed something about the history of the shroud that nobody anticipated. He found pieces of insects, hairs, dust and many other pieces of material but most importantly, there were several different kinds of pollen. Remember, this man was not only a police officer and a photographic expert; he was also a botanist (a man who was knowledge-able of plant life). Fortunately, pollen keeps its physical shape for thousands of years, and of all of the pollens he identified there were six types of pollen that were unique to the Jordan Valley. Some people would say that Max was chosen by God because he was not only an expert in photography but he was also educated in botany (a person knowledgeable regarding plant life). This changed Max Freid's mind regarding the authenticity of the shroud. Within 120 hours, Max went from a skeptic to a believer. The pollen proved that the shroud was not a European forgery; at one time, it positively was in the area of Jerusalem. This evidence cast much doubt on the 14th-century European forgery theory.

He also had a news conference and announced his findings and stated he now believed that this was, in fact, <u>the burial cloth of Jesus Christ.</u>

After 120 hours of collecting the data, the Turin Commission completed their investigations and it was concluded with a brief ceremony by the church, which included <u>a prayer</u>, and the shroud was put away and the scientists began to pack up their equipment and collected data to go back to their own countries and analyze their findings. When the American portion of the Turin Commission arrived back in the United States, almost immediately there was a descending voice among the four hundred scientists from around the world, and because this person commanded so much respect his accusation must be addressed. He was an American and his name was Dr. Walter McCrone. As a forensic scientist, he was well respected. He had gained much notoriety when he was given an artifact to determine, if a particular map was authentic or not. A museum had purchased this map, which was believed to be a 1442 map, and it clearly showed the coastline of Eastern America. This map, if it was authentic, would predate the Columbus arrival to America by fifty years. Unfortunately for the people that bought the map, Dr. McCrone proved that the ink used to print this map wasn't in use until 1920, making the map a forgery. Dr. McCrone's job on the Turin Commission was to examine the supposed <u>blood areas</u> of the shroud and determine what was the red stuff made of. Was it blood?

After a few weeks, the heads of the commission contacted Dr. McCrone and he surprised everyone and declared that the <u>red stuff</u> on the shroud was not blood. He claimed it was iron oxide, a type of paint made from pulverized rust of iron. Furthermore, he claimed that this material (iron oxide) was not available until the Industrial Revolution in the 1700s. Some experts were quick to discredit this accusation because iron oxide had been in use for thousands of years as paint. The men from the commission asked Dr. Mc Crone, what test did he perform to substantiate or prove that it was iron oxide? His reply was he didn't have to run any tests; he could tell just by looking at it that it was, in fact, iron oxide. They did not accept his <u>opinion</u> and demanded that he run tests to prove his accusation. He reluctantly said he would. They finished their communications with an agreement that Dr. McCrone should conduct tests to verify and substantiate his <u>observations</u>. This event stimulated interest of other men who wanted to get involved in the truth about the blood sample. Now there were other scientists that were eager to participate in the study, but unfortunately they had a very small amount of material to work with, only seven Pico grams of this material. A Pico gram is one millionth of a gram. Dr. McCrone's sample was much larger, so at this point there were two separate blood investigations going on at the same time. Dr. McCrone, who had the largest sample, and Dr. John Heller, who was working with a much smaller sample.

Sometime later, Dr. McCrone claimed to have conducted tests that verified his accusation. When they asked Walter McCrone if they could examine the lab test that he claimed proved that the red stuff was, in fact, iron oxide, he refused and he would only give them <u>the results of the test</u>. Dr. Heller, along with many others, was suspicious. Dr. McCrone was willing to give the commission <u>the results of the test</u> but not the test themselves. At that point the decision was made to retrieve the test samples from

Dr. McCrone and they were giving to Dr. John Heller and after his team ran tests, they reached a totally different conclusion. The first thing Dr. Heller's team did was to do the same test Dr. McCrone claimed to have performed and got totally different results. They wanted to get together with Dr. McCrone and work out their differences. They also wanted to see the lab tests Dr. McCrone claimed he had performed, but he refused to meet with them or to give them the test that he supposedly ran and only repeated <u>his personal opinion</u>, that the red stuff was iron oxide. Dr. Heller and his team went on and conducted several different tests and proved that the red stuff was not only blood, but human blood as well. Three times in as many years Dr. McCrone was invited to debate his differences with the opposition team, and three times he refused.

The other team that was being led by Dr. John Heller went on to prove by three separate tests, all accepted by the American judicial system (the court systems) that the red stuff was not only blood but was, in fact, human blood. What was Dr. McCrone's thinking or what his motivation were for lying, we will never know, because he died shortly after the turn of the century, standing by his false and inaccurate claim. These are the facts that are known regarding the shroud. First, Dr. Robert Bucklin, deputy medical examiner and forensic pathologist of Los Angeles County in California, said #1: Irrespective (which means it doesn't matter) of how the image was made, there is adequate information on the shroud to state that they are anatomically (physiology) correct. The pathology (the study of damage to the body) and physiology (the normal functions of the living organism) are unquestionable and represent medical knowledge unknown 150 years ago. #2: That the wounds depicted <u>on the man on the shroud</u> are more accurate than the Bible's account. #3: The image on the shroud is a negative, not a positive, unknown before photography was invented, roughly in the year 1850. The Turin Commission went on to find the following facts regarding the shroud: #4: The man on the shroud has a swollen nostril, a swollen eye, a cut lip (the

Roman guards beat Jesus terribly), #5: and cut marks around his head (this was because the Roman guards slammed a crown of thorns on Jesus' head, mocking him as a king). This is recorded in the Bible. #6: He was beat with a type of whip known to be used by the Romans two thousand years ago. #7: There is a puncture wound to his chest (this was caused by Roman soldiers after Jesus died, which is recorded in the Bible), and #8: An indentation on his shoulders showing he carried something very heavy right before he died. (This was caused by Jesus being forced to carry his own crucifixion cross to be crucified with until he collapsed and a Samaritan helped Jesus by carrying his cross for him.) This is also recorded in the Bible.

#9: Crucifixions are accomplished by driving spikes through the wrists, convulsing the thumbs into the palms of his hands (which is reflected on the shroud) and cramping the chest, making it impossible for Jesus to breathe. They were not in the palms of his hands, as the Bible says, and #10: The spikes in his feet enabled Jesus to relieve the pressure on his median nerve in his arms by standing on the spike driven through his feet, which allowed Jesus to breathe temporarily. #11: This up-and-down motion causes two streams of blood to run down his arms (which are visible on Jesus' arms) ten degrees apart (just like the man on the shroud). #12: Because <u>the material of the shroud would curve over the outside of the legs, the image of his legs</u>

would be distorted and they are. #13: Because the material would touch his forehead, nose, chin and chest and not the eyes, mouth and neck, there would be a shroud body distance factor (and there is). #14: There are no earth pigments, capillarity or any brush marks on the shroud, proving it is not a painting or drawing. #15: The image is 100-percent visible with the exception of a thin line at the heel of his feet. The absence of this part of the heel can be explained because people who walk without shoes (as Jesus did) acquire a callous at the heel and over time it cracks and dust or dirt accumulates in the cracks, which would block or prevent the energy that was emulated from Jesus' body from reaching the shroud material (that's what caused the absence of this part of Jesus' feet). #16: Everything according to the Gospels that was experienced by Jesus is represented on the man on the shroud. #17: Except the location of the spike in the wrist, rather than the palms of his hands, the image on the shroud was correct <u>and the Bible account was wrong.</u> <u>#18: Even with the technology of today, it would be impossible to make an image with all of the qualities that the shroud possesses</u>. #19: That the critics of the shroud thought it was a European forgery <u>and it has pollen unique from the Jordan Valley, proving it was at one time in Jerusalem.</u> #20: <u>Of the four hundred scientists</u> and technicians who worked on the mystery of the shroud, there <u>was only one man</u>

<u>with an opposing opinion and he was</u> <u>proven wrong with scientific tests</u>. #21: After 120 hours of examining and gathering the scientific data in 1978 and over t- 40 years later, no one could discredit the authenticity of the shroud.

#22: So overwhelming was the evidence of the shroud's authenticity that at the Turin Commission's final meeting and press conference in 1981, the reporters repeatedly asked each group of scientists after they presented their findings if this was proof that the image was Jesus, and each scientist said they didn't know and could only repeat what evidence was uncovered. Finally, the head of the commission stood up and said, "You can believe that the shroud was made by elves in the black forest if you want to, <u>but we don't have Jesus to compare it to</u>, so therefore it is impossible for us to say that it is the burial cloth of Jesus." <u>This was a fair and unbiased scientific statement;</u> however, by listening to the rest of the statement, it should be convincing of the shroud's authenticity. Finally, a man asked the head of the Turin Commission, was there any proof <u>that it wasn't</u> the burial shroud of Jesus, <u>and his reply was no.</u> With that one word, many skeptics were forced to rethink their opinion.

With literally no evidence disproving the authenticity of this cloth, there can only be one logical conclusion. <u>This is, in fact, the burial cloth of Jesus Christ.</u> When all the evidence was in proving the authenticity of the shroud, another group of scientists wanted to take one more crack at either proving or disproving the authenticity of the shroud. The final step was a carbon-14 dating of the material of the shroud. <u>How old was the material of the shroud?</u> The Vatican was asked to give some scientists a piece of the cloth to carbon date it in order to find out how old the shroud was. The Vatican asked these people how much of the shroud they required to run this carbon dating test. The scientists said they required a piece that was one inch wide and one foot long. The Vatican refused because they did not want to sacrifice that much of the burial cloth of Jesus Christ.

A few years later, the same scientists returned to the Vatican and explained to them that the C-14 dating process was improved and now they only required a piece that was only a quarter-inch wide and six inches long. The Vatican reluctantly agreed to cut and remove this much of the shroud for the C-14 dating process, expecting with all the other information that had already been collected and verifying the authenticity of the shroud that the test would be another verification of its authenticity. This seemed like it would only be another confirmation of the authenticity of the burial cloth of Jesus. However, much to everyone's shock, after conducting the test that group of scientists stated that the test indicated the shroud was only one thousand years old, making it much too young or not old enough to be the burial cloth of Jesus Christ. This announcement stunned the entire world and this accusation was recorded in newspaper headlines all around the world. Skeptics were elated. However, within about a six- or seven-year period, another scientist was examining a picture of the sample of the shroud that the Vatican had submitted to the scientists for the C-14 dating test and made a discovery. The sample that was given to the scientists to conduct that C-14 dating test had additional threads on it that were not part of the original shroud. This obviously would have affected the correct dating of the material of the shroud. He went to the labs that conducted the C-14 test and he asked them, how did they arrive at the conclusion that the shroud was only one thousand years old? <u>They admitted</u> that there were several tests made of the sample of the shroud that the Vatican sent to them and those tests disagreed with each other and were spread over an eight-hundred-year period. This fact alone should have told those scientists that there was something wrong with their findings, and their conclusions were incorrect. The scientists that made the discovery of the different threads that were on the sample of the shroud that the Vatican sent them asked the scientist that conducted the carbon-14 dating test, "How did you arrive at the conclusion that the shroud was only one thousand years old?" They said that of all the different tests they performed on the sample of the shroud that the Vatican gave them, the results of those dates were spread over an eight-hundred-year period. The man who discovered the different threads on the sample of the shroud that the Vatican gave them asked, "How did you arrive at the conclusion that the shroud was only one thousand years old?" They said that there was a cluster of three dates between the ages of nine hundred to eleven hundred years old, so we disregarded all the other test dates and we use those three test dates to make our determination that the shroud was only one thousand years old. The fact that the other tests of the shroud were spread over an eight-hundred-year period should have told those scientists that there was something wrong with their conclusion of the dating of the shroud. Then the scientists that discovered the additional threads on the sample they received from the Vatican of the shroud asked the scientist that conducted the test, *"Are you going to stand by your decision that the shroud is only one thousand years old?"* The man replied, "Because of this evidence, we must admit our conclusion regarding the shroud was incorrect." This admission of their mistake was never widely publicized, and the damage to the reputation of the authenticity of the shroud will be remembered. However, the medallion of King Abgar proved the shroud was two thousand years old. Someday another sample of the shroud should be tested and it will be <u>correctly dated</u>. I can understand why the Vatican is reluctant to cut another piece of the burial shroud of Jesus Christ for further testing. They trusted the scientists once and the scientists made a mistake, so why trust them again? How many times should the Vatican cut this sacred piece of material for further testing, <u>just to satisfy the public of its authenticity?</u> My personal opinion is <u>one more time</u>. Why?——- <u>For Christ's sake</u>!

CONCLUSION

This brings us to review what this book is all about. #1: The first thing that was covered was how all of these churches came about. Between the_- Holy Bible that combined both the Old Testament, which is the religion of Judaism, and the New Testament, which contain Christianity, and the American right of freedom of religion, this has created all of these pseudo-Christian religions. #2: This book, using the words of Jesus Christ, destroyed the cliché that the Holy Bible is the Word of God. #3: The scientific evidence in the universe that <u>seems</u> to indicate that there is, in fact, <u>a God</u>, #4: and how life was first created on earth also indicating that there is a God. #5: And the scientific evidence regarding the shroud, which proves that Jesus was resurrected and proves there must, <u>in fact, be a God</u>. #6: Christians need and deserve their own Bible.

I thank you for giving me your time and allowing me to share with you what I have learned from the scientists that I was privileged to work with who also believed in God. God bless you, and I hope we will see each other in heaven.

I would like to leave you with some advice. Christianity is not only different than other religions, but it can also be dangerous to share. As Jesus said to his apostles as he sent them out to do his work in the book of Matthew, chapter 10, verse 16: "Be as wise as a serpent but peaceful as a dove. Be a Christian but also be careful. Don't share your Christianity with everybody. Listen to them first and determine if your Christianity is safe to share. Because of your Christianity, some individuals will consider you vulnerable."

Good luck and <u>God bless YOU.</u>